STUDY GUIDE

The Consequences of Ideas

An Overview of Philosophy

R.C. Sproul

LIGONIER MINISTRIES
Renew your Mind.
LIGONIER.ORG | 800-435-4343

421 Ligonier Court, Sanford, FL 32771
Email: info@ligonier.org

Writer: Robert Barnes

Printed in China.

1

The Beginnings of Philosophy

MESSAGE OVERVIEW

I. Introduction to *The Consequences of Ideas: An Overview of Philosophy with R.C. Sproul*
   A. All activities relate to the nature of ideas
   B. Goal: A brief introduction to philosophy, both the concepts and persons involved in Western philosophy,

II. The beginning: May 28, 585 B.C.
   A. The solar eclipse on this date was predicted by Thales of Ionia
   B. The age of pre-Socratic philosophy began with Thales

III. The One and the Many
   A. Universe and university
   B. What provides unity in the midst of diversity? Is it cosmos or chaos?
   C. Thales, who was in search of the answer to these questions, also stated "What is ultimate reality?"
   D. Metaphysics
   E. What is the purpose (*telos*) for the universe?
   F. *Arche* or essence
   G. The ultimate reality for Thales: Water
      i. It explained ontology or being
      ii. It explained the relationship of solids, liquids, or gases
      iii. It explained motion: Water appeared to be hylozoistic

STUDY QUESTIONS

1. What are the goals of this series?

2. With whom did Western philosophy begin?

3. What civilization is it associated with?

4. What main questions did they attempt to solve?

APPLICATION

1. What does your culture think is the most basic material that forms the universe?

2. What are the main questions your culture seeks to answer?

3. How well do you answer these questions from a biblical perspective?

2

Pre-Socratic Philosophers

MESSAGE OVERVIEW

I. Key Participants in Pre-Socratic Philosophy
   A. Anaximenes of Miletus (547 B.C.): Air is the answer to the three questions of being, essence and motion
   B. Anaximander of Miletus: No definite substance is "the" answer, so it must be indefinite
   C. *Apeiron*: a boundless, ageless and infinite material, also known as the "5th Essence"
   D. Greek philosophy only attained monotheism after many years, while Hebrew philosophy/theology began with this idea
   E. The being Anaximander conceived was not personal, but purely transcendent

II. Pre-Socratic Categories
   A. Monists: All reality is one (pantheism). God is "the One"
   B. Pluralists: All reality is various, like a multitude of "seeds." Democritus best summed up this position with his belief that all reality was made up of tiny particles, also called atoms
   C. Corporeal and Incorporeal Monists: Either one substance or one spiritual entity make up reality
   D. Corporeal and Incorporeal Pluralists: Either many particles or many spiritual particles make up reality

STUDY QUESTIONS

1. What is the difference between Monism and Pluralism?

2. How do the corporeal and incorporeal factors affect these positions?

APPLICATION

1. Using these categories, how would you explain the beliefs of your culture?

2. Do you know various groups who hold some of these positions? Who are they?

3. What is the biblical view of these ideas?

3

Heraclitus, Parmenides, and Zeno

MESSAGE OVERVIEW

I. The Philosophy of Popeye

II. Philosophy and Being: Language is not possible without grammatical use of "being," but it is nevertheless mysterious

III. Heraclitus, Parmenides and Zeno
   A. Heraclitus of Ephesus: Everything that exists is in a state of flux—whatever is, is changing. "You cannot step into the same river twice" was his motto. He was also a Monist, but saw whatever was the "one" as being dynamic
   B. Parmenides of Elea: "Whatever is, is", or, that which truly exists is not in flux. This was counter to Heraclitus by saying that if objects are truly in constant flux, they cannot be said to "be" anything. And even if they were once "something", they are not now because the object changed to something different
   C. The history of philosophy is a continuance of the debate between these two men
   D. Zeno of Elea (490 B.C.): A pupil of Parmenides who made the *reductio ad absurdum* argument famous. His main opponents were the pluralistic Pythagoreans. His four arguments against motion were the stories of Achilles and the tortoise, stadium (half-way argument), flying arrow, and moving rows

STUDY QUESTIONS

1. What does Heraclitus teach about reality?

2. How did his teaching compare to Parmenides?

3. How did Parmenides critique Heraclitus?

4. What made Zeno famous?

APPLICATION

1. Do you see reality as "everything stays the same," or "everything changes"?

2. What modern cult has picked up on Zeno's philosophy (Hint: Mary Baker Eddy was its founder)?

4

Socrates

MESSAGE OVERVIEW

I. Introduction: The Danish Gadfly and Socrates
   A. Lived in Athens (circa 468-397 B.C.) in a critical time of Greek civilization
   B. "The unexamined life is not worth living"
   C. In Socrates' life, Sparta defeated Athens, leaving Athens weakened economically and philosophically. They were disillusioned with religion and ready to accept skepticism as the best option

II. The Environment of Socrates: Sophists and their Impact
   A. With the decline of Greek culture, the sophists, with whom Plato did combat, grew less and less sage-like and more superficial
   B. The sophists were itinerant teachers, who, for a fee, would give you their ideas and education. Their goal was to develop artful rhetoric which would persuade—whether it was true or not
   C. The society was just beginning to use the jury system of conviction, so the place of professional oration was growing more important

III. The Environment of Socrates: Protagoras and Gorgias
   A. *Homo mensura*: Man is the measure of all things
   B. Gorgias was an early skeptic who said that "good" is what advances your own self-interest

IV. The Mission of Socrates
   A. He analyzed and challenged the presuppositions of his culture by engaging the people in dialog and by asking them questions, called "The Socratic Method"
   B. Plato's records of Socrates demonstrate this method of Socrates' moving people from their superficial sophism to truth

C. Key ideas of Socrates: True knowledge comes through the admission of ignorance
D. Key Moral concern was virtue and the basis of it
E. Socrates was killed because he was charged with atheism and the intellectual seduction of the youth of Athens

STUDY QUESTIONS

1. What was the condition of the culture in which Socrates taught?

2. What were the contemporary teachings he opposed?

3. How and why did he die?

APPLICATION

1. Is there anyone in your life who has been a "Socrates", asking you hard questions about your basic beliefs? How did you respond?

2. What are the presuppositions of our culture that need to be questioned?

5

Plato (Part 1)

MESSAGE OVERVIEW

I. Introduction: R.C.'s visit to his cousin in Philadelphia

II. Plato's Beginnings
   A. Born in 427 B.C., 28 years old when Socrates died
   B. Plato was so nicknamed because of his broad shoulders
   C. His parents were of noble descent

III. Plato's Accomplishments and Ideas
   A. Stared a school called "The Academy." Over the door of the school was a sign "Let none but geometers enter here," showing the broad nature of his schooling and to denote his belief that reality was math-like
   B. Plato's "Theory of Ideas" or "Forms" denotes him as an idealist and a realist
      i. Idealist: Truth is ultimately formal, not material. It exists in another realm, a spiritual one. This enables us to know that a chair is indeed a chair, distinguishing it from horses and couches, because chairs remind us of the perfect essence/idea of "chairness" which exists elsewhere
      ii. Realist: The ideas are actually real
   C. Problem created by an unreal, imperfect physical world (receptacles) and a "real" and "good" ideal world: Reality is bad, the physical world is dirty and corrupt, only the spirit realm is good

STUDY QUESTIONS

1. How old was Plato when his teacher died?

2. From what section of society did he come?

3. How was Plato an idealist and a realist at the same time?

APPLICATION

1. Are there parts of the church that still think that the world is completely evil and only that which is spiritual is good?

2. How does the Bible speak against these ideas?

3. How do you deal with this struggle as you try to live in the world without completely rejecting it, and yet grow in personal holiness?

6

Plato (Part 2)

MESSAGE OVERVIEW

I. Introduction: Karl Barth's lectures on F. Schleiermacher (1768-1834)

II. Plato's Metaphysics or Ontology: How do we know?
  A. Epistemology and the "*Theory of Recollection*"
  B. Plato's goal was to understand knowledge
  C. Plato's *Cave* (From *Republic*, Book 7)

III. Plato's Understanding of the Soul and Mind
  A. The soul contains the knowledge of these pre-existent, innate ideas. It is eternal, but is obscured by the body
  B. *A Priori*: Knowledge prior to experience
  C. Plato was influenced by the Pythagoreans, who believed a doctrine known as the "Transmigration of the Soul", which we know today as the doctrine of reincarnation
  D. The body as the prison of the soul and the problem of imperfect sense perception
  E. Education: getting out of your body the information that is already there
  F. *Meno* and the art of leading questions

IV. Saving the Phenomena
  A. What is the foundation of science?
  B. How do we deal with anomalies?
  C. What does it mean to expand your paradigm?

V. Plato and the Good
   A. Is Plato's "Good" his god?
   B. Justin Martyr saw Plato as under the influence of the divine *logos*

STUDY QUESTIONS

1. How did Plato claim we obtain knowledge?

2. How did he and Meno prove this?

3. What did Plato mean by "saving the phenomena"?

APPLICATION

1. Does the Bible teach we are a "blank slate" when born, or do we have innate knowledge?

2. How do Christians integrate new information or ideas into their worldview?

3. Does the Bible affect your views on science, math, sex, or art? Why or why not?

7

Aristotle (Part 1)

MESSAGE OVERVIEW

I. Ideas or Events
   A. A false dichotomy
   B. The consequence of ideas

II. Aristotle and His Impact
   A. A student of Plato, with the pet name of "The Brain", was passed over as leader of the *Academy*. This began a relational rift that became a philosophical one.
   B. Parapatetic dialog was the rule in Aristotle's *Lyceum* (founded in 335 B.C)
   C. Aristotle disagreed with Plato and sought unity rather than the tension of the "objects" and "ideals" existing at once
   D. Most famous student of Aristotle: Alexander the Great, who tried to Hellenize as many people as possible through conquests, lived out the philosophical idea of unity

III. Aristotle's *Theory of Substance*
   A. All things exist as a primary substance, in contrast to Plato's belief that objects were secondary
   B. Matter and Form: attempted to solve the problem of being and becoming
   C. Every substance contains both matter and form, with form giving the object its being. Matter changes, or becomes. These two factors make an object unified
   D. Actuality and Potentiality: relates to qualities of form and matter (in that order)

E. Substance and accidens: every physical object has substance (with matter and form) and accidens (external, perceivable qualities of an object)
F. Application: The Roman Catholic Church explains transubstantiation by using Aristotle's theories
G. You could not have pure matter, but you could have pure form. This was Aristotle's idea of God

STUDY QUESTIONS

1. What were the differences between Aristotle and Plato that R.C. mentioned?

2. Who was the most famous student of Aristotle?

3. How did this student apply his master's teaching?

4. How does the Roman Catholic Church apply Aristotle's teaching on accidens?

APPLICATION

1. While we are not forbidden to learn from philosophies, when the Bible speaks to a matter, we are not to seek a "better" answer elsewhere.

2. Give an example of the church rejecting the biblical wisdom in favor of philosophical wisdom.

3. In what areas do you tend to heed the advice of philosophers or counselors instead of the advice of Scripture? Ask God to give you wisdom in this area.

8

Aristotle (Part 2)

MESSAGE OVERVIEW

I. Review of Last Lecture

II. Aristotle and His View of God
   A. God is defined as the *Unmoved Mover* or the *Uncaused Cause*
   B. How do all the independent entities gain unity?
   C. Aristotle's god is the source of all motion (or change), but how could the source of motion be motionless?
   D. The Moth and the Flame
   E. Aristotle's god is not personal or even similar to the Judeo-Christian God, although theologians such as Aquinas have used his views
   F. *A Priori* and *A Posteriori*

III. A Distinction: Realism (*res*) and Nominalism (*nomina*)
   A. Are ideas real?
   B. Universals are not things, but names. Aristotle was a nominalist
   C. Truth: Conformity between the mind and the thing
   D. Logic and the knowing process
   E. Logic: The *organon* (instrument) of all science and intelligent discourse
   F. Application: Today, logic and reason are under assault
   G. The general and the particular, or, the subject and the predicate
   H. The law of non-contradiction

STUDY QUESTIONS

1. Describe Aristotle's god.
2. How did Aristotle define truth?
3. What was the place of logic in his system?

APPLICATION

1. How similar is your God to Aristotle's god?
2. Compare his view of God to that presented in the Bible, particularly Exodus 2:23-25. How are they different? Similar?

9

Plotinus and Neo-Platonism

MESSAGE OVERVIEW

I. Another Period of Skepticism

II. Stoicism and Epicureanism: What was the secret of living the happy life?

III. Christian Philosophical Ideas
   A. God is unified in the Trinity
   B. History is focused by divine providence

IV. Neo-Platonism (3rd century) as a response to Christianity
   A. Plotinus (203-270) rejected Christianity and sought to provide an option
   B. As with the gnostics, Plotinus thought real truth came through mystical intuition, not through the physical world or our senses
   C. The "contemplative life" is the way to true wisdom
   D. Christian mysticism is different from Plotinus; mysticism: it stops with "communio"
   E. Plotinus said we should move from sensation to contemplation to *communio* to *unio*
   F. Plotinus said God is "The One", but tried to avoid pantheism. You cannot know the One, except through *via negationis*, or, the way of negation
   G. Plotinus, from *Enneads*, VI. ix. 3.4.
   "The intelligence is a thing, and belongs to Real Being: the One is not anything, but prior to all things, neither is it a kind of Real Being. Real Being possesses a character comparable to Shape, the intelligible shape of the Real: the One is not shaped even by intelligible shape. For that Principle which generates all things cannot be anything of them all. It is not a thing, it is not quality, it is not quantity, it is not Intelligence nor Soul. It does not move, and yet it is not at rest, either in space or in time: it is the Uniform-absolute,

or rather the Formless as being prior to all Form and prior to Motion and Rest. For these last are characters of Real Being, and make Reality manifold. If it be asked, why the One, having no movement is not at rest, we answer, because only to a Being must one or both of these predicates apply. A stationary object is at rest, but is no Rest; and so also, if the One be at rest, Rest will be added to it as an accident, and it will no longer remain simple. Even to name it the Cause, is to predicate an accident not of the One, but of ourselves; it signifies that whilst the One abides within itself we have something derived thence. He that would speak exactly must not name it by this name or by that; we can but circle, as it were, about its circumference seeking to interpret in speech our experience of it, now shooting near the mark, and again disappointed of our aim by reason of the antinomies we fine in it."

H. Tillich and Plotinus: Is God nothing?
I. Plotinus and his influence on Augustine

STUDY QUESTIONS

1. What was the impact of early Christian philosophy on the Hellenistic world?

2. What were the two skeptical philosophical movements that arose during the New Testament times?

3. What was Plotinus; estimation of Christianity?

4. What option did he provide?

APPLICATION

1. Do Plotinus' beliefs remind you of other philosophies in your culture?

2. As you read the quote above, does it strike you how confusing reality would be without the God of the Bible?

10

Augustine

MESSAGE OVERVIEW

I. Introduction to St. Augustine (354-430 A.D.)

II. His Contributions to Theology
   A. Soteriology
   B. Ecclesiology

III. His Background
   A. An early life of debauchery
   B. Philosophically dabbled in Manichaeism

IV. The Battles he fought
   A. Donatist controversy
   B. Pelagian controversy
   C. Skeptical controversy
      i. Sense perception
      ii. Illustration of boat oar
      iii. The content of perception is part of reality
      iv. The reliability of sense perception and the formal level of knowledge
      v. The goal of knowledge: beatific happiness
   D. Apologetics and the existence of God
   E. Creation *Ex Nihilo* and the divine fiat

V. Neo-Platonism (3rd century) as a response to Christianity
   - Plontinus (203-270) rejected Christianity and sought to provide an option

STUDY QUESTIONS

1. What were the two areas of theology that Augustine impacted?

2. Which area did the Protestant church use as its basis?

3. Who emphasized the other area? What was Augustine's background like?

4. What do we know about his conversion?

5. With which controversies was he involved?

6. Who responded to Augustine's impact on philosophy?

APPLICATION

1. What is most impressive to you about Augustine?

2. Augustine would not have been able to have been a member of any conservative Protestant church in the world today. He believed in baptismal regeneration, prayers for the dead and to the dead, and many other practices we see as plainly unbiblical today. Why do we honor him as a great theologian?

3. Is it fair to question whether he was Christian or not?

11

Anselm

MESSAGE OVERVIEW

I. Christian Thinkers Dominated the First Millennium

II. St. Anselm, Archbishop of Canterbury (1033-1109 A.D.)
  A. His major works
    i. *Cur Deus Homo?* Why the God-man? Why was the Atonement necessary for the salvation of mankind?
    ii. *Monologium* developed his *credo ut intelligam,* his reasons to believe in God. "If anything exists, it exists by the means of something or by the means of nothing" was a simple basis for his discussion
    iii. *Proslogium* developed his controversial "Ontological Argument" for God's existence
  B. The Ontological Argument
    i. God is that being than which no greater being can be conceived
    ii. If you are thinking of a lesser being, or suggest that He does not exist, then a greater being can exist than that
    iii. Gaunilo's Response: The greatest island
    iv. Anselm's Response: An island is not a being
    v. Presupposition: Self-existent being(s) cannot NOT exist. We can imagine island not existing. But not something with being

III. Necessary Being
  A. A being who is both logically necessary and ontologically necessary
  B. Anselm is leading us to the logical necessity of a real being. The impossibility of the contrary, when applied to the existence of God, is a powerful argument.

STUDY QUESTIONS

1. What was the subject matter of Anselm's major works?

2. Explain in your own words his argument for God's existence.

3. Is God a necessary being?

APPLICATION

1. If you could write a book, what would it be on?

2. What is the most helpful argument for God's existence to you?

3. How does Romans 1, which teaches that all people truly know God exists, but are in denial, impact your presentation of the Gospel?

12

Aquinas (Part 1)

MESSAGE OVERVIEW

I. Thomas Aquinas (1225-74 A.D.) is Known as the Angelic Doctor of the Roman Catholic Church

II. Dr. Aquinas: The Good and the Bad
   A. Dr. Francis Schaeffer critiqued him as separating nature and grace.
   B. Islamic philosophers had sought to construct a synthesis out of which developed the "Double Truth" theory. Double Truth teaches that a proposition can be true in science, yet false in religion. Or, true in philosophy and false in science. This application of Aristotle's philosophy was the first separation of nature and grace
   C. It is against the theory of "Double Truth" that St. Aquinas was responding
   D. But what Aquinas did affirm is that there are certain truths we learn from nature and certain truths we learn from special revelation. These do not contradict
   E. Special and general revelation: distinct categories, but not separate ones. They are distinguished in order to show their true unity in God
   F. *Articulus Mixtus* (mixed articles)

STUDY QUESTIONS

1. What biographical facts about Aquinas did you learn from the message?

2. How did Islamic philosophers integrate Aristotle's philosophy into their apologetics?

3. How did Aquinas distinguish between natural and special revelation?

APPLICATION

1. Do you know people who say that only the Bible has truth in it and the world is only full of lies?

2. How does this show a misunderstanding of general revelation?

3. There is a tension between the two extremes of discarding all truths outside the Bible and accepting without question all science has to offer. Which error are you more likely to make?

4. How can a Christian stay in balance on this issue?

13

Aquinas (Part 2)

MESSAGE OVERVIEW

I. Review of Thomas Aquinas, the "Angelic Doctor" (1225-1274)

II. His Main Contribution: Natural Theology
   A. Was (and is) attacked by many Protestants because they assume a departure from a dependence on biblical revelation
   B. Aquinas qualified his understanding of natural theology, attempting to guard it from such objections
   C. Meditate: God reveals Himself indirectly, via creation
   D. Incomplete: God reveals Himself, but not completely
   E. True: However limited, natural theology is a true revelation of God
   F. Analogy and the Person of God
      i. Analogical: between the two extremes of univocal and equivocal
         a. Necessary Being: Ontologically necessary, and neither dependent, derived or contingent
         b. Logically necessary
      ii. Univocal: Good dog verses good man—radical unity
      iii. Equivocal: Bald narrative versus bald men—radical difference
   G. The analogy of being: The language we use about God is the language of analogy. There are multiple points of similarities between, for instance, God's fatherhood and human fatherhood. Thus, we can talk about God as Father

STUDY QUESTIONS

1. What is Natural Theology?
2. How much can we learn about God from creation?
3. Is what we learn true?
4. What are the limits of Natural Revelation?

APPLICATION

1. Consider the implications if what we learn from nature about God is not perfectly true.
2. How could God justly judge the rebellious pagan if he never had an accurate picture of God (Rom. 1)?

14

The Renaissance Revolution

MESSAGE OVERVIEW

I. The Renaissance of the 13th and 14th centuries

II. "Ad Fontes" or How the Renaissance Changed the World
   A. At first, studies of the Bible were under-emphasized. But later in the Renaissance it became key, with the rise of Erasmus
   B. The Renaissance brought a change to the way education was envisioned. Theology was no longer the queen of the sciences—her handmaiden philosophy ascended to reign in this time
   C. Teleology: The study of "why" was banished from the science realm
   D. Scientific Revolution of the 15th and 16th centuries
      i. Geocentricity
      ii. Heliocentricity
   E. Scientific Method
      i. Induction
      ii. Deduction
   F. Technology and instrumentation
   G Age of Exploration
   H. Money and the moral question of usury
   I. Changes in the church: Simony and nepotism

STUDY QUESTIONS

1. Did the Renaissance occur before or after the Reformation?

2. Name three ways the Renaissance changed the world for the better.

3. Name three ways the Renaissance changed the world for the worse.

APPLICATION

1. Would you have enjoyed living in the Renaissance? Why or why not?

2. How do the presuppositions created by the Renaissance affect the Protestant church today?

15

Descartes

MESSAGE OVERVIEW

I. The Renaissance was a transition to the Modern Age, which began in the 17th century, also called the Age of Reason or the Enlightenment

II. Rene Descartes (1596-1650)
   A. As with many philosophers, Descartes was also a mathematician. This was normal until philosophy became high specialized
   B. Descartes was at the center of the most optimistic time in history
   C. *Fides Implictum*: Authorities that were previously united were in conflict
   D. Descartes wanted certitude, not the upheaval of the 16th century
   E. "A Discourse on Method": His first book on intuition (clear and distinct ideas) and deduction unveiled the way he would seek truth
   F. Laws of Immediate Inference: All men are mortal vs. Some men are mortal
   G. "In the subjects we propose to investigate, our inquiries should be directed not to what others have though, nor to what we ourselves conjecture, but to what we can clearly behold and with certainty deduce..."
   H. A systematic process led him to prove he was doubting. It was "For someone to doubt, you must have thought. If you think, you must have something to do the thinking. Therefore, *cogito ergo sum*: I think, therefore, I am."
   I. Self-consciousness is the starting point of all philosophical investigation

STUDY QUESTIONS

1. What was Descartes' background prior to philosophy?

2. How did he attempt to attain certitude in the midst of skepticism?

3. Explain his process for attaining his foundation for philosophical exploration.

APPLICATION

1. Descartes was a world-class doubter. Do you ever doubt the essentials of Christianity, your own existence, or other fundamental ideas?

2. If so, what do you doubt?

3. If not, why do you not doubt?

4. How do you attain “cognitive rest” when facing hard questions about God and the universe?

16

Descartes and "Cause and Effect"

MESSAGE OVERVIEW

I. Philosophical Assumptions about Cause and Effect
   A. A trip to the doctor: What caused the problem?
   B. The assumption of cause and effect was challenged by Descartes
   C. What is thought? Are ideas physical or not?
   D. Extension and non-extension
   E. Interactionism

II. God, the 20th Century, and Cause and Effect
   A. What are the consequences of these ideas on Christianity?
   B. The modern worldview believes in a mechanistic universe
   C. A transfer of energy
   D. Primary and secondary causality
   E. Malebranche and Occasionalism: No mind/body interaction, it is only the power of God making it apparently true

STUDY QUESTIONS

1. What does cause and effect describe?

2. How did Descartes challenge it?

3. What consequences did his thoughts have on Christian philosophy?

4. What is the difference between primary and secondary causality?

5. Explain in your own words Occasionalism.

APPLICATION

1. What makes Occasionalism attractive?

2. Do you know some people who take the biblical idea of God's sovereignty too far?

3. What are the results of this error?

17

Leibniz

MESSAGE OVERVIEW

I. Gottfried Wilhelm Leibniz (1646-1716)
   A. Only a part-time philosopher, inventor of calculus, historian and jurist
   B. Sought to demonstrate the necessity of God, but was not an occasionalist

II. Leibniz's Thought and Theory
   A. Monadology: Each tiny "monad" expresses the whole universe by virtue of perceiving it. God programs these monads, thus explaining their behavior apart from their effect on each other, which Leibniz believed did not occur
   B. Law of Pre-Established Harmony: The programming God gives the monads from the foundations of the earth
   C. Theodicy: A justification of God in the area of the problem of evil
      i. Metaphysical "Evil": An imperfection given to finite begins
      ii. Physical "Evil": Natural havoc, including sickness and floods
      iii. Moral Evil: Sin
      iv. These three have a linear flow
      v. God has created the "best of all possible worlds," and in this way, God is free from guilt
      vi. Voltaire's *Candide* was a response to this belief
      vii. Problem with this theory: It does not justify God and there is a better world coming, according to Scripture

STUDY QUESTIONS

1. What was the primary profession of Leibniz?

2. What is the relationship of mathematics and philosophy?

3. What is a monad?

4. What was Leibniz's view of God?

5. What question or challenge was Leibniz trying to answer?

APPLICATION

1. Do we currently live in the best of all possible world? Why or why not?

2. What part does God's sovereignty in everything play in the "bestness" of this world?

3. Or the next world?

18

Pascal

MESSAGE OVERVIEW

I. Introduction to Blaise Pascal (1623-1662)
   A. Scientist, theologian, and passionate believer in Christ
   B. Had a personal, powerful experience with Christ
   C. Resisted the Jesuit movement, as involved with *Jansenism*, a revival of Augustinian thinking

II. The *Pensees* of Pascal
   A. Spoke of man as the paradox of creation, having the highest grandeur, but greatest misery as well
      i. Highest grandeur: can contemplate self, nature, and God. Particularly, we can contemplate a better life for ourselves
      ii. Greatest misery: We cannot experience that better life
   B. Pascal's Wager: Why believe in the existence of God?
      i. Everyone must make a decision: to restrict your decisions to secular, or to incorporate the aspect of the spiritual into your life
      ii. You are betting your life that there is no God as you choose to live a God-less life
      iii. If you lose this bet, you die having lived a rather empty, purposeless life
      iv. If you live a purposeful, God-centered life, doing good to others and praising those who do the same, and there is no God, then you have lived a good life, but have not lost anything
      v. So, protect your downside—live in such a way that can maximize your gains and minimize your losses
   C. Criticisms of the Wager
      i. This argument, like many of his reflections, is not complete
      ii. Assumes nihilism is not true, and that life actually has meaning
      iii. You actually do lose some things in the Christian life

STUDY QUESTIONS

1. What Roman Catholic movement did Pascal oppose?
2. After his conversion, what movement did he support?
3. In your own words, articulate Pascal's Wager. What is the valid criticism of this argument?

APPLICATION

1. Before you were a believer, how would you have responded to Pascal's argument?
2. What is the best "argument" you know for the existence of God?
3. How helpful are these arguments?

19

Locke

MESSAGE OVERVIEW

I. Introduction to Rationalism and Empiricism
   A. Rationalism
   B. Empiricism
   C. What is the ultimate source of truth?
   D. Three ways to use the term "rationalism"

II. Introduction to John Locke (1632-1704)
   A. An empiricist who wrote on political theory, impacted many with ideas of representative government
   B. Locke's epistemology is his most important philosophical contribution
   C. John Locke was a physician, not a speculative thinker, but very common sense oriented
   D. He was an enemy of conceptualism, that is, the belief that whatever is rational and conceivable must exist. Illustration: Bright red polar bears

III. Locke's theories about truth
   A. Correspondence theory of truth: the truth is that which corresponds to reality
   B. This is an ida that is under assault in the postmodern world, for truth is preference in our culture
   C. *Tabula rasa*: We are born with a mind without inclinations
   D. *A priori* and *a posteriori*: Locke argued for the latter
   E. Locke claimed knowledge begins with particulars and the universals are results of multiple, individual experiences we put together
   F. The mind has innate abilities to receive data and discriminate it
   G. For Locke, the question of how knowledge arrives to us, whether through experience or through the mind is key. It will remain so throughout the history of philosophy.

STUDY QUESTIONS

1. What are rationalism and empiricism?
2. What are three kinds of rationalism?
3. Why was Locke opposed to conceptionalism?
4. What was the main question Locke wanted answered?

APPLICATION

1. How does your culture attack the correspondence theory of truth?
2. From a biblical perspective, what is truth and how do we know it?

20

Crisis in the 18th Century (Part 1)

MESSAGE OVERVIEW

I. With What is philosophy Concerned?
   A. Metaphysics
   B. Epistemology

II. "Saving the Phenomena"
   A. The philosopher and scientist of antiquity were trying to make sense of the diversity and unity witnessed in nature
   B. What is really out there and how do we understand it with certitude?
      i. Subject/object problem
   C. Deduction and Induction
      i. Induction: Moving from the particular to the universal
      ii. Deduction: Moving from the universal to the particular
         a. All men are mortal
         b. Socrates is a man
            • Socrates is mortal
      iii. If logic is limited, how do we attain certitude?
      iv. Paradigm shift occurs when you have too many exceptions to what was thought to be a foundational rule

III. The 18th Century
   A. The world is getting bigger
   B. The world is getting smaller

STUDY QUESTIONS

1. Define metaphysics and epistemology.
2. What is the subject/object problem?
3. Define inductive and deductive.
4. What is a paradigm shift?

APPLICATION

1. Have you ever had a crisis in your religion or philosophy?
2. If yes, how was it resolved?
3. If no, what keeps you from questioning things more?

21

Crisis in the 18th Century (Part 2)

MESSAGE OVERVIEW

I. Theories of Matter and Substance
   A. Some have said that "Trees are 90% air"
   B. The make-up of the atom confirms this, even taking it further

II. How do We Know What is Blue?
   A. Roger's shirt
   B. Is blue a reality or only a perception, existing in the mind alone?

III. Revisiting Accidens, Substance and Essence
   A. Primary qualities
   B. Secondary qualities
   C. There are real metaphysical realities, and we perceive the substratum of being
   D. A mixed perception is because of primary and secondary qualities, according to Locke

IV. George Berkeley (1685-1753)
   A. Wanted to save God from the philosophy of formal materialism
      i. Was an Anglican theologian
      ii. Had a great impact on Jonathan Edwards

STUDY QUESTIONS

1. How do we know what is blue?

2. Define accidens, substance, and essence.

3. Define primary and secondary qualities.

APPLICATION

1. Is blue a reality or only a perception, existing in the mind alone?

2. How do we know the difference between blue and red?

3. To the extent that we are created in the image of God, how much of God's qualities or abilities do we share?

4. How do these communicable attributes form categories to help us see things as God does?

22

Berkeley and Empiricism

MESSAGE OVERVIEW

I. The Disadvantage of Empiricism
   A. A built-in limitation with respect to philosophical certainty
   B. You cannot observe all the data necessary to make absolutely certain conclusions
   C. 18th century empiricism thus ended in skepticism

II. George Berkeley's Idealistic Empiricism
   A. If a tree falls in the forest and nobody is there to hear it fall, does it make any sound?
   B. *Esse est percipi*: To be is to be perceived
   C. Does matter disappear? Is everything an illusion? Not at all. But we cannot have real being without perception
   D. Thus, all is real, because God, the Great Perceiver, hears and sees all. Reality is in the mind of God. "In Him, we live and move and have our being."
   E. Now, God is not important, but is absolutely necessary for science to exist

III. Berkeley vs. Correspondence Theory of Locke
   A. Essences and extensions
   B. The difference between metaphysics and physics
   C. All qualities are secondary, only God perceives the essence

IV. Berkeley's Correspondence Theory
   A. Reality is as God perceives it, and the world is an extension of God's thought
   B. Hume brings the supreme crisis of knowledge by attempting to remove all hope of knowing the essence of reality

STUDY QUESTIONS

1. From this lecture and previous ones, what ideas made empiricism a "next step" for philosophy?

2. What is the disadvantage of it?

3. What did Berkeley do to combat atheistic philosophies?

APPLICATION

1. Does Bishop Berkeley's idea make sense?

2. Does it have any scriptural support?

3. Does the Bible attempt to prove a certain philosophical perspective, or does it assume one?

23

Hume (Part 1)

MESSAGE OVERVIEW

I. Introduction to Hume and Causation
   A. The common use of "because"
   B. David Hume (1711-1776): His major books were *An Inquiry concerning Human Understanding (1748)* and *Dialogues concerning Natural Religion* (published post-mortem)
   C. Individuation: How are we able to sort and discriminate data?
   D. How does sensation relate to thought? And which is more powerful? Hume would say sensation
   E. Memory: Points out the weakness of thought compared to experience. It is related to the sensations and dependent on their intensity or vivacity
   F. Side note: Jonathan Edwards' sermon *Sinners in the Hands of an Angry God*

II. Causality
   A. The grass is wet because the rain fell on it. But how do you know this? How do you know that when one thing follows the other, this means the latter was caused by the former?
   B. *Post Hoc* fallacy
   C. Ordinary Relationship or Ordinary Connection: Is this a necessary connection? Leibniz and Occasionalists would say no and argue for a direct, immediate work of God
   D. Hume distinguished between a *customary* and a *causal* relationship, and in doing so raised questions about causality
   E. This stabs the heart of many causal arguments for Christianity, the existence of miracles, and the necessity for the existence of God

STUDY QUESTIONS

1. How did Hume say we gain knowledge, through sensation or thought?

2. What were the questions that Hume raised about causality?

3. What effect do these questions have on the classical arguments for Christianity?

APPLICATION

1. How do you think Hume's arguments cause trouble for classical arguments for God's existence, such as the cosmological or teleological?

24

Hume (Part 2)

MESSAGE OVERVIEW

I. Hume and the Problem of the Cue Ball
   A. The actions which go into making a pool shot are an example of matters of causation Hume was raising
   B. Contiguous actions
   C. Hume's argument: causation is assumed, but not proven. A customary, not necessary, association
   D. Hume is an empiricist. He believed we only see relative reactions, not actual causation

II. Has David Hume Defeated the Reality of Causality?
   A. Causality is a formal statement or law
   B. If something does not have a cause, then it would be improper to call it an effect
   C. Many have drawn the conclusion that Hume has disproven causality itself. That was not his point. What he is skeptical about is our ability to see the precise cause of whatsoever happens. And in this, Hume is correct
   D. We do know that if the wetness of the grass is an effect, then something necessarily caused it. If I say "I did not perceive creation", that does not mean and Hume has not proven that it did not happen

III. Hume and *Dialogues Concerning Religion*
   A. When there is a claim of a miracle, a natural explanation is always more reasonable—the ordinary is more likely than the extraordinary
   B. Hume said that the customary effect following death is not resurrection, but death. The probability quotient would be astronomical

C. There are many interesting arguments for Christ's deity, but they are mute compared tot he event of the resurrection. If Jesus died, and stayed dead, we are fools
D. Unique event: The weak part of Hume's argument against miracles is that it misunderstands uniqueness

STUDY QUESTIONS

1. What does empiricism mean?

2. Using the analogy of a pool game, explain the problem of causation that Hume was raising. What is the difference between customary and necessary causation?

3. How did Hume attack religion?

4. How does R.C. critique Hume's thinking?

APPLICATION

1. Do Hume's ideas concern or scare you?

2. Do you think R.C. has successfully dealt with Hume's ideas?

3. Why or why not?

4. What would you say to Hume if you could have talked to him about his beliefs?

25

The Enlightenment (Part 1)

MESSAGE OVERVIEW

I. Introduction to the Enlightenment
   A. The 18th century Enlightenment in Europe has led to a serious detriment of spiritual thinking in today's Western Europe
   B. The Enlightenment marks the triumph of Erasmus over Luther, or humanism over reformation
   C. The Enlightenment was strongest in Germany, England and France
   D. This was not a monolithic movement; there were a variety of beliefs
   E. They did share a common approach to knowledge

II. Analytical Method
   A. The scientific paradigm was applied to every area of life and science
   B. Issaic Newton was a Christian scientist during this time, seeing his vocation as holy
   C. Logic of Facts: Does data yield an observable pattern?
   D. Our society has rejected this, especially when it comes to theology
   E. This "Logic of Facts is not a bad thing, properly used
   F. The problem comes when we use this tool in places it was not intended to be used or where it is not useful
   G Example: Montesque and his analysis of government
   H. With triumph of humanism, new forms of government would be key in creating a new race

STUDY QUESTIONS

1. What did the different factions of the Enlightenment have in common?

2. What is the "analytical method"?

3. What is the "logic of facts"?

4. What was the main goal of the Enlightenment?

APPLICATION

1. How does the Enlightenment affect your culture today?

2. Are its effects growing or lessening?

3. Has the Enlightenment affected the way you read the Bible? Explain.

26

The Enlightenment (Part 2)

MESSAGE OVERVIEW

I. The Enlightenment and the Mind
   A. The Enlightenment believed in the power of the mind
   B. The church, believing in a fallen man, was seen as a roadblock to development of mankind

II. The Philosophers of the Enlightenment
   A. Rousseau, was a theist, but against the church
   B. Voltaire and his opposition to God
   C. The French Encyclopedists: Totally opposed religion of any type, espousing spontaneous generation and other absurd ideas

III. Natural Religion
   A. A basic religious movement that encouraged toleration above all
   B. Historically speaking, at the same time America was experiencing the Great Awakening
   C. Deism: A god exists, but now is separate from the universe and only revels himself though natural revelation. Thus, they sought to get rid of the Bible
   D. Natural Law and Natural Theology flourished during this time
   E. Jean-Jacques Rousseau (1712-1778): "Man is born free and everywhere is in chains".
   F. Edwards believed that the Bible proves man's fallen nature, but also natural reason must account for the universality of human failure
   G Rousseau believed we are born virtuous, but we are spoiled by improper government. The natural, independent nature of humanity creates exploitative relationships where it is profitable to manipulate others. This destroys

individuals and makes us become whatever the ones in power make us. Rousseau believed we need a contract or covenant between rulers and ordinary people. This thinking had an enormous impact on America and the formation of our government. It also led to skepticism.

STUDY QUESTIONS

1. What have we learned about Rousseau, Voltaire, and the French Encyclopedists?

2. How did they oppose Christianity?

3. Define natural religion. Describe how Rousseau's philosophy affected his political ideas?

APPLICATION

1. How do our philosophies or religious ideas affect our politics?

2. How did Rousseau's ideas affect our own government?

3. How did the Bible effect the formation of the United States government?

27

Kant (Part 1)

MESSAGE OVERVIEW

I. Introduction to Immanuel Kant (1724-1804)
   A. Philosophy is reckoned by Kant's impact on the science
   B. Philosophy flows by tension moving to resolution through synthesis
   C. The history of philosophy pre-Kant can generally be divided into rationalism and empiricism. Parmenides, Plato, Augustine, and Leibniz would be seen as rationalists. Heraclitus, Aristotle, Aquinas, Bacon, Locke, and Hume would be Empiricists
   D. Post-Kant: He created a new paradigm. Existentialism, pragmatism, relativism, pluralism, idealism, all these and more flow from references to Kant
   E. *A priori* and *a posteriori*
   F. Kant was awakened from his "dogmatic slumber" by the work of David Hume, who had seemingly destroyed the ability to know

II. The Transcendental Method
   A. If there is knowledge, how do we know it? Sense experience is the starting point for Kant
   B. Kant disagreed with those who believed in innate ideas, such as Descartes. But he distinguished between *a priori* knowledge (prior to experience) and innate ideas
   C. Kant's "sausage grinder": Sensations going into mental categories
   D. How do we tell and define time?
   E. How do we distinguish or discriminate sensations?
   F. Space and time are pre-intuitions
   G. What comes out of the meat grinder? Knowledge

III. The Nature of Truth
    A. Truth is a judgement
        i. *a priori*
        ii. *a posteriori*
        iii. analytical
        iv. synthetic
    B. This creates a crisis in philosophy that plagues us today

STUDY QUESTIONS

1. Whose work motivated Kant to rethink his philosophy? Why?

2. What were Kant's fundamental beliefs?

3. What is the difference between *a priori* and *a posteriori*?

4. What is "Kant's Sausage Grinder"?

5. What is the nature of truth, according to Kant?

APPLICATION

1. Can you think of another person who has had the kind of impact on his/her discipline as Kant?

2. If truth is simply a "judgment call", what impact would that have on the way someone would decide about ethics or religion?

28

Kant (Part 2)

MESSAGE OVERVIEW

I. "You Can't Get There from Here"
   A. Kant seemed to build a wall between this world (phenomenal) and the postulated noumenal (spiritual) realm
   B. Three dwellers of the noumenal realm
      i. Essences
      ii. Self: Defined by Kant as "a transcendental aperception of the ego"
      iii. God
         a. Arguments for his existence
         b. Refutations of those arguments
         c. Antinomies

II. Critique of Practical Reason
   A. Kant said that even though we cannot know God exists, we must assume it for practical reasons
   B. The moral argument for God's existence
   C. Categorical imperative
   D. What would have to be true for ethics to be meaningful? There would have to be a god of some kind, one who is just and powerful enough to make the wicked pay for their crimes, perfect in his understanding of the evidence, and he must be righteous and incorruptible. Omnipotent, omniscient, righteous, holy: sounds like the God of the Bible

STUDY QUESTIONS

1. Define "phenomenal" and "noumenal." How are they different?

2. Did Kant believe God exists? Why or why not?

APPLICATION

1. What are some of the reasons people give for not believing in God?

2. In right and wrong?

3. Why are ethics meaningful to Christianity?

29

Hegel

MESSAGE OVERVIEW

I. The 19th Century and Hegel
   A. "The Phenomenology of Mind"
   B. Tension was placed on the phenomenal realm
   C. A philosophy of history emerged in the 19th century
      i. Dialectical view of history or "Dialectical Idealism"
      ii. Dialectical Materialism was the title for Marx's philosophy
      iii. Very simply, Hegel is difficult to understand

II. Kant's Wall Created Distinctions Between God and His Work
   A. Immanentism or *diesitzeheit*
   B. Transcendence
   C. Hegel said the noumenal could get over Kant's wall by God's revelation of Himself via nature

III. Hegel and History
   A. In all areas of human experience, we find a process taking place that involves tensions that are overcome in history. This is known as "The Triad" or *Aufgehoben*
      i. Thesis
      ii. Antithesis
      iii. Synthesis: This becomes the next thesis, continuing the pattern
   B. Examples of this cycle can be seen in music and art
   C. History is an unfolding of the "absolute spirit". History does not simply reveal God, it is God
   D. History is the incarnation of God
   E. History is the revelation of God
   F. All revelation is natural or general because all history is God's experience of Himself and is Divine, according to Hegel

G. Hegel's ideas were dialectical, having many seemingly contradictory ideas which they said could be resolved through the experience of history

IV. The Religious-Historical school of the 19th century was essentially evolutionary

STUDY QUESTIONS

1. How did Hegel say we could get over "Kant's Wall"?

2. In Hegel's opinion, who is God and what is His relationship to history and nature? What main questions did Hegel attempt to solve?

APPLICATION

1. Does Hegel's language remind you of any philosophical or religious movement in your culture? If so, explain.

2. What part of Hegel's philosophy seems to make the most sense? Why?

30

Marx

MESSAGE OVERVIEW

I. Introduction to Karl Marx
   A. Marx's father joined the Lutheran church out of business interests, and this hypocrisy changed Marx's view of God forever
   B. Marx was a student of Hegel, but disagreed with Hegel about what was most real, either material possessions or ideas. Thus was founded Dialectical Materialism, counter to Hegel's Dialectical Idealism
   C. Class struggle

II. Homo Faber or Homo Sapiens?
   A. Alienation of labor: We become slaves as we chase increased wages given by the owners of the factories
   B. Marx encouraged violent revolution, with common men bringing about "equality" with the owners of factories by revolt
   C. Labor theory of value versus supply and demand
   D. State ownership of means of production versus private ownership

III. Critique of Law and Religion
   A. Substructure
   B. Superstructure
   C. Religion is the opiate of the masses, invented as a way to exploit the masses
   D. Utopian eschatology of Marxism

STUDY QUESTIONS

1. What changed Marx's view of religion?

2. Summarize Marxism in your own words.

APPLICATION

1. Did an event in your youth change your view of God? What was it?

2. Can you be a Christian marxist, based on Acts 2:44-47? Why or why not?

31

Kierkegaard

MESSAGE OVERVIEW

I. Introduction to Soren Kierkegaard (1813-1855)
   A. The gadfly of the Danes
   B. A passionate, Christian philosopher

II. The Stadium
   A. Aesthetic
      i. Epicurean Hedonists
      ii. Abstractionists, or "Eggheads", who remained uninvolved
      iii. These received the majority of Kierkegaard's wrath
   B. Ethical
      i. An advanced stage, but not the highest
      ii. A desire for morality and truth is good, but not the best
   C. Religious and *Fear and Trembling*
      i. *Fear and Trembling*, a story of Abraham and authentic religious life
      ii. "And Abraham rose up early in the morning"
      iii. "The Temporary Suspension of the Ethical"
      iv. "A Leap of Faith"
      v. "The Paradox of the Moment"
      vi. "Moment" and Decartes' point in linear space

III. Insights from various characters and works
   A. Job: "Though He slay me, yet will I trust Him"
   B. The clown and the burning theater
   C. The rebel and the pitiful king: "More wood!"
   D. *Sickness Unto Death* (1849) loneliness of the mourning believer like unto the suffering of someone critically ill
   E. Kierkegaard and Hegel: *The Concept of Irony* and subjective truth

IV. Kierkegaard's Legacy: Our response to God should be one of unrestrained passion toward our beloved

STUDY QUESTIONS

1. Where was Kierkegaard from?
2. What was his concern for his people?
3. How did he manifest that concern?
4. What was the subject matter of *Fear and Trembling*?

APPLICATION

1. Kierkegaard's desire was that people live authentic lives. Do you ever feel like you are not living a "real" life, not feeling either pain or joy very deeply?
2. What makes modern men (particularly Christians) drift toward this numb way of living?
3. Noting the emotions expressed in the Psalms, is it a sign of a spiritual person to have few emotions? Or to be extravagantly emotional?

32

Nietzsche

MESSAGE OVERVIEW

I. Introduction to Atheistic Existentialism and Friedrich Nietzsche (1844-1900)
   A. Was convinced that Christian virtues instilled weakness
   B. Authentic human existence
   C. The father of Nihilism, which teaches that there is no ultimate meaning to human existence
   D. Popularized the "Death of God" idea

II. Biological Heroism
   A. *Also Sprach Zarathustra* (1883-1892) is his most famous work, but he had many significant writings, beginning with *Die Geburt der Tragodie* and ending with *Der Antichrist*
   B. To be *Ubermensch* or Superman was the personal goal for Nietzsche, and he believed all should strive for this goal
   C. "Will to Power" or "King of the Hill"
   D. Why would someone who did not believe in values or truth encourage people to pursue power?
   E. "Dialectical Courage" was the cardinal virtue of Nietzsche
   F. The Greek ideals of Apollo and Dionysius: Nietzche praised the latter
   G. Believed that history was one of eternal occurrence: "They shoot horses, don't they?"
   H. Died insane, infected by syphilis, and signed his letters "The Crucified One"

STUDY QUESTIONS

1. What was Nietzsche's opinion of Christianity?

2. What is nihilism?

3. What is the primary virtue of Nietzsche's worldview?

4. Why did Nietzsche say God died?

APPLICATION

1. Have you ever met someone who claimed to be a nihilist?

2. What would it take to be a consistent one?

3. Why is nihilism more consistent than most false philosophies?

4. What is its fatal weakness?

33

Sartre and Heidegger

MESSAGE OVERVIEW

I. These are the Two Most Important Philosophers of the 20th Century
  A. Both were existentialists
  B. Both were taught by Husserl, a Jewish philosopher

II. Jean Paul Sartre (1905-1980)
  A. Combined philosophical ability with literary skill
  B. Major work was *Being and Nothingness* (1943)
  C. Atheistic Existentialist, opposed to Kierkegaard
  D. World War I impacted the spirit of optimism of the 19th century, and World War II destroyed it, leaving a deep sense of despair. The "beat generation", led by Jack Kerouac, continued to articulate this despair into the 70s

III. The Ideas of Sartre
  A. "Existence precedes Essence"
  B. No unifying principle, reality is irrational, nothing fits together in a meaningful way
  C. Human existence: The defining trait is *subjectivity*. We are not *objects*, but *subjects*. The chief attribute of a subject is *will*, specifically *free will*
  D. If God is sovereign, then man cannot be free, according to Sartre. Restriction of freedom is the ultimate sin. If man is free, God cannot exist
  E. Argument against God's existence: If the God of the Bible exists, with all His higher attributes, then humans cannot exist, since our chief attribute is freedom
  F. *The Cosmic Voyeur* would dehumanize us, reducing us to objects. Therefore, God does not exist
  G. *No Exit*: A philosophical play by Sartre that explains his ideas about "staring"

H. A "useless passion"
I. *Nausea*

IV. Martin Heidegger (1889-1976)
A. Atheistic Existentialist
B. Biographical information includes affiliation with Nazi regime

V. The Ideas of Heidegger
A. *Sein* and *dasein*
B. Where do you live?
C. Finitude, caring, anxiety, but no reason for being
D. *Geworfenheit*: Having been thrown or hurled into existence
E. He ends with a philosophy of despair, one which inspired Albert Camus to say that the only thing left to consider was how and when to die—suicide
F. Ernest Hemingway was a popular (and consistent) proponent of these ideas

STUDY QUESTIONS

1. What did Sartre and Heidegger have in common?

2. On what did they differ?

3. What were the key ideas of each philosopher?

4. Why do these philosophies lead to despair?

APPLICATION

1. What truths are present in these philosophies, and to some extent, all existential philosophies?

2. How is it tempting for Christians to not "live in the moment"?

3. Do you experience the feeling of being "hurled into existence"?

4. Is it wrong for a Christian to feel this way?

34

Russell

MESSAGE OVERVIEW

I. Introduction to Bertrand Russell (1872-1970)
   A. Focused on the relationship between logic and mathematics
   B. British philosopher of mathematics, popular writer against atomic weapons and Christianity. In his later years, he wrote *Why I Am Not a Christian*

II. Russell's Objections to Historic Theism
   A. Critiqued the cosmological argument by questioning causation as John Stuart Mill did, and popularized the idea of infinite regress. But they both erred concerning the law of cause and effect
   B. The problem of evil: If God is good and powerful, then how does sin and suffering exist? But suffering is linked to God's goodness and power, not contradicted by it
   C. The Parousia Delay: Jesus made prediction that did not come to pass, specifically noting Matthew 24. See *The Last Days According to Jesus*, by R.C. Sproul for a comprehensive response to this objection

STUDY QUESTIONS

1. What questions about the veracity of the Christian faith did Russell raise?

2. How does R.C. answer these objections?

APPLICATION

1. What is the best argument you know against the veracity of the Bible?

2. The existence of God?

3. Playing the "devil's advocate," argue against the particulars of the Christian faith, and give biblical, rational responses to these arguments.

35

Modern Philosophers

MESSAGE OVERVIEW

I. Broad Picture of Philosophical Inquiry in the 20th Century
   A. The school of Positivism introduced by A. Compt birthed much of modern philosophy
   B. Three stages of cultural development
      i. Infancy: religious inquiry, a query into myth
      ii. Adolescence: abstract philosophical inquiry
      iii. Adult: scientific, empirical inquiry
   C. A.J. Flair and Anthony Flew are two British philosophers who propagated these ideas
   D. The Law of Verification
   E. Are our discussions about God meaningful, or is our language about God simply emotive?
   F. The Falsification Principle: the Law of Verification cannot be verified. It fell under its own weight
   G. Pragmatism, formulated by John Dewey and George Pierce
      i. No such thing as value, only values
      ii. No such thing as truth, only truths
      iii. Emphasis on being rather than becoming and the illustration of sending his child to school in Boston
   H. F. Schaeffer and "true truth" fought positivistic ideas
   I. Illustration of John Rock and "Does it work?"
   J. What does it profit a man, if he gains the whole world, but loses his own soul?
   K. Pluralism and Relativism
   L Linguistic analysis or the philosophy of language
      i. Witgenstein: Meaning is defined by customary usage, so the task of the philologist is to clarify meaning. In a sense, this brings us back to square one, attempting to define our terms (again)

CLOSING COMMENTS

The idea that has the deepest consequences of all is that words have meaning because God has spoken them. We passionately commit ourselves to God and His truth, being diligent to express His truth in what we do and say.

STUDY QUESTIONS

1. What are the three stages of growth in philosophical dialogue?

2. What is the Law of Verification and why does it fail?

3. How does the philosophy or study of language by Witgenstein take us back to the beginning of philosophical inquiry?

APPLICATION

1. In state-run colleges and universities, many of the philosophies we have studied are taken as completely true, with little discernment shown in plumbing the truth of them. What steps should one take to discover the truth and error present in a series of ideas?